Affirmations for Kids and Parents:

Helping Families Connect Better Through Talking, Writing and Pictures

By Dr. Junior Harrism III, MD, MS

Dear Mom and Dad,

I want to thank you both for all your support and opportunities through-out my years. For example, when I turned 16 years old and had a car waiting for me, for getting me a tutor when I needed one, allowing me the opportunities to explore different sports and travel the world, and so much more. I owe you two for giving me a great foundation in life. Also, being an adult now, I realized that I took a lot of things for granted as a kid and I thank you two for having patience with me.
Thank you for believing in me, Mom and Dad.

Love you,
Your son, Little Junior

P.S. I wanted to thank both of my brothers Jason and John. I love you and thanks for all your support.

Also, I want to thank everyone for supporting this project/book.

This book is designed to encourage kids and parents to develop a better understanding of each other by sharing thoughts and feelings.

ISBN: 979-8-218-35049-9
Library of Congress Control Number: 2024900744

First printing, 2022.

www.theeducationmovement.com

www.dimesacademy.com

Instructions for Kids and Parents

1. Turn Off Electronics: Before starting, please turn off all electronic devices. This helps everyone focus on the book and each other without distractions.

2. Dedicated Time: Each child should have their own copy of the book. Parents and children should sit together, creating a special time for reading, writing, and talking.

3. Engage Fully: Read the book together, discussing each section and question. Encourage open conversation about the answers.

4. Writing Together: Both parents and children should write down their answers to the questions in the book. This is a shared activity that promotes reflection and bonding.

5. Expressive Affirmations: When you come across affirmations, feel free to speak them out loud. You can be as expressive and loud as you want. The key is to feel the power of your words.

6. Review and Reflect: After writing your answers, take time to review them. Look at the pictures and read aloud what you wrote. This reinforces the messages and strengthens the connection between parent and child.

These instructions are designed to create a meaningful and engaging experience for both kids and parents, fostering communication and personal growth through the power of affirmations.

Who are you? (parents and children talk)

1.Child:

2.Parent:

1.Child:

2.Parent:

1.Child:

2.Parent:

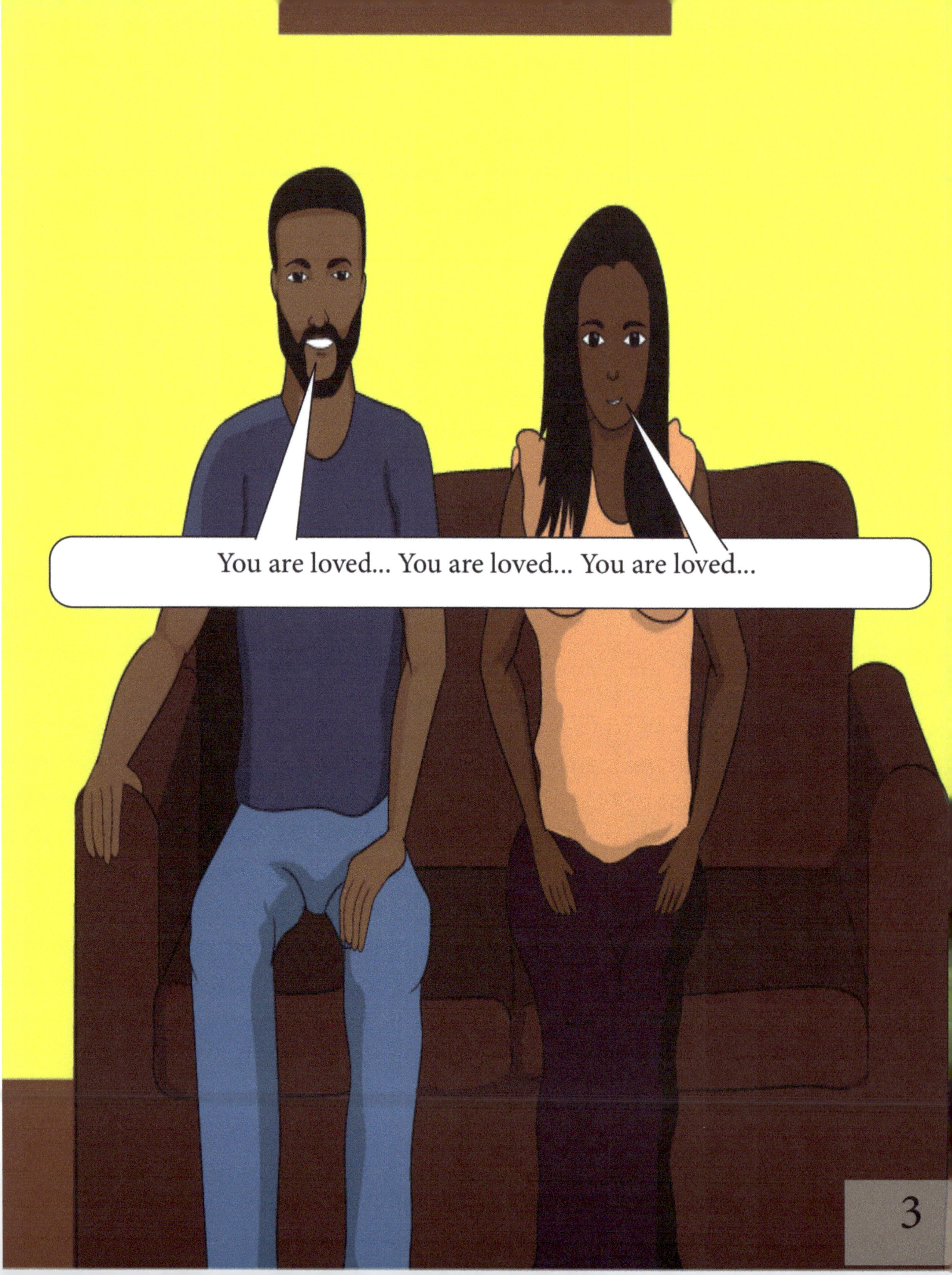
You are loved... You are loved... You are loved...

Who loves You? (parents and children talk)

1.Child:

2.Parent:

1.Child:

2.Parent:

1.Child:

2.Parent:

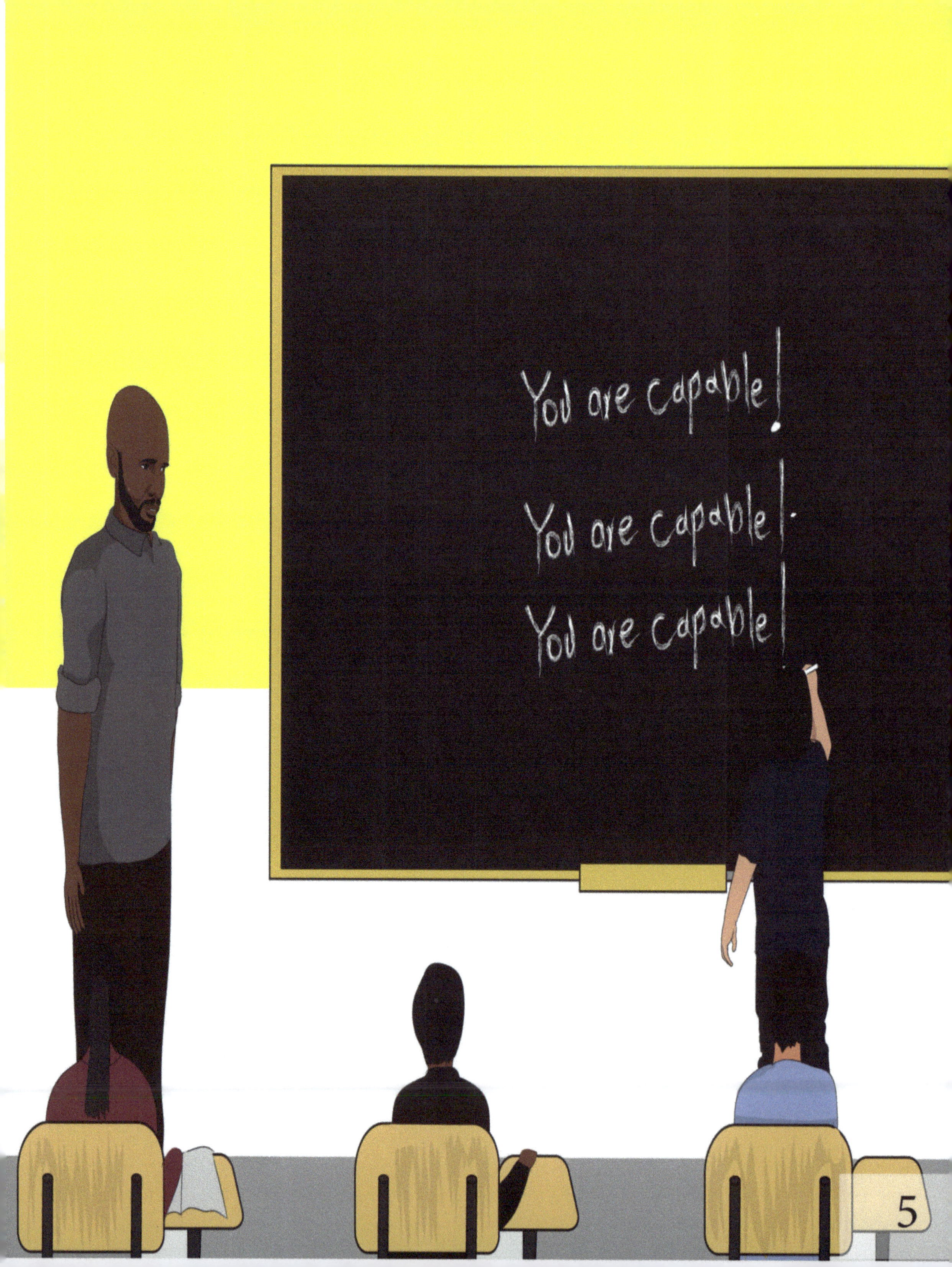
You are capable!
You are capable!
You are capable!

What are you capable of? (parents and children talk)

1.Child:

2.Parent:

1.Child:

2.Parent:

1.Child:

2.Parent:

How are you unique and smart? (parents and children talk)

1.Child:

2.Parent:

1.Child:

2.Parent:

1.Child:

2.Parent:

What does it take to be leader? (parents and children talk)

1.Child:

2.Parent:

1.Child:

2.Parent:

1.Child:

2.Parent:

How are you enough?(parents and children talk)

1.Child:

2.Parent:

1.Child:

2.Parent:

1.Child:

2.Parent:

How are you amazing? (parents and children talk)

1.Child:

2.Parent:

1.Child:

2.Parent:

1.Child:

2.Parent:

How special am I? (parents and children talk)

1.Child:

2.Parent:

1.Child:

2.Parent:

1.Child:

2.Parent:

How brave am I? (parents and children talk)

1.Child:

2.Parent:

1.Child:

2.Parent:

1.Child:

2.Parent:

What do you want to invent? (parents and children talk)

1.Child:

2.Parent:

1.Child:

2.Parent:

1.Child:

2.Parent:

How strong and powerful am I? (parents and children talk)

1.Child:

2.Parent:

1.Child:

2.Parent:

1.Child:

2.Parent:

I am a believer... I am a believer... I am a believer

What do you believe? (parents and children talk)

1.Child:

2.Parent:

1.Child:

2.Parent:

1.Child:

2.Parent:

What have you learned today? (parents and children talk)

1.Child:

2.Parent:

1.Child:

2.Parent:

1.Child:

2.Parent:

I love my epidermis... I love my epidermis... I love my epidermis

27

What do you love about your epidermis/yourself?
(Parents and children talk)

1.Child:

2.Parent:

1.Child:

2.Parent:

1.Child:

2.Parent:

28